Inside the NFL

THE
DALLAS
COWBOYS

BOB ITALIA
ABDO & Daughters

Published by Abdo & Daughters, 4940 Viking Drive, Suite 622, Edina, Minnesota 55435.

Printed in the United States.

Cover Photo credit: Wide World Photos/Allsport
Interior Photo credits: Wide World Photos: page 4-13, 15-17, 19-21, 23, 24, 27, 28

Edited by Kal Gronvall

Library of Congress Cataloging-in-Publication Data

Italia, Bob, 1955—
        The Dallas Cowboys / Bob Italia.
        p. cm. — (Inside the NFL)
Includes bibliographical references and index.
Summary: A brief history of the Dallas Cowboys football team, one of the top teams in the National Football League.
ISBN 1-56239-461-4
1. Dallas Cowboys (Football team)—Juvenile literature. [1. Dallas Cowboys (Football team)] I. Title. II. Series: Italia, Bob, 1955- Inside the NFL.
GV956.D3I85   1995
796.332'64'097642812—dc20   95-16694
                                                                              CIP
                                                                              AC

CONTENTS

The Cowboy Dynasty

In just over three decades, the Dallas Cowboys have become one of the National Football League's (NFL's) top teams. They have won four Super Bowls, and have developed some of the most outstanding players in NFL history.

Quarterback Roger Staubach looks for a receiver downfield.

Quarterback Roger Staubach was Dallas' first big star. He guided them to their first Super Bowl victories. Then came along running back Tony Dorsett, who ranks among the top career rushers and who holds a number of league and team records.

In the early 1990s, Dallas reassembled another football dynasty with many star players. Quarterback Troy Aikman shattered rookie passing records his first year, and has become one of the NFL's best passers. Running back Emmitt Smith won three consecutive rushing titles—and still has his sights set on more. Even wide receiver Michael Irvin stands to set a number of receiving records before his career is over. And then there is Deion Sanders, who signed with the Cowboys in 1995.

Dallas still has a young team. Though they did not capture their third-straight Super Bowl title in 1994, the Cowboys will be looking for more championships in the near future.

Tony Dorsett ranks among the NFL's all-time career rushers and holds many league and team records.

The Dallas Rangers

The NFL came to Dallas, Texas, in 1952. The team was known as the Dallas Texans. The Texans had some talented players, but in their first season, they only won one game. They beat the Chicago Bears before 3,000 fans in Akron, Ohio. At the end of the season, the Dallas Texans were out of business—the first team to ever drop out of the NFL.

Coach Tom Landry (left), Jerry Rhome (center) and general manager Tex Schramm look over Rhome's contract as Dallas' quarterback.

Professional football did not return to Dallas until 1959. Texas multimillionaire Clint Murchison, Jr., wanted to bring a professional football team back to Dallas. At the same time, another Texas multimillionaire, Lamar Hunt, formed the American Football League (AFL)—including a team named the Dallas Texans.

Murchison hired the former general manager of the Los Angeles Rams, Texas "Tex" Schramm, to run his team. Schramm worked as an assistant director of sports programming for CBS-TV. He moved to Dallas in November 1959. Schramm and Murchison had to build their team with free agents and acquired players because the 1960 NFL college draft had already taken place.

Dandy Don

What Schramm needed most was a quarterback. Both Hunt and Schramm wanted the 6-foot 3-inch, 200-pound, two-time All-American from Southern Methodist University (SMU), "Dandy" Don Meredith. Hunt had already drafted Meredith for the AFL. But Meredith wanted to play in the NFL.

To make sure that no other team picked Meredith, Murchison called on Chicago Bears owner George Halas. As a favor, Halas drafted Meredith for the Bears and traded him to Dallas for a third-round draft pick in 1962.

Murchison used the same tactics to sign another great player, running back Don Perkins. The Baltimore Colts drafted Perkins, who was later traded to Dallas for a ninth-round draft pick in 1962.

Using this strategy, Schramm and Murchison built a team. On December 28, 1959, Schramm hired Tom Landry as the head coach of the Dallas Rangers. Then on January 28, 1960, the NFL voted to award a franchise to Clint Murchison.

Quarterback Don Meredith, left, and coach Tom Landry review films of the Cowboys' prior games.

From Rangers to Cowboys

In early 1960, Schramm organized the team and hired a staff. Then in March, Schramm changed the team's name to the Dallas Cowboys.

To be competitive in their first year, Landry and Schramm wanted an experienced quarterback while Meredith improved his skills. The Cowboys signed former Washington Redskins quarterback Eddie LeBaron.

The Dallas offense was not good. Even worse, Don Perkins suffered a season-ending injury. After losing 10 straight games, the Cowboys tied the New York Giants 31-31. They lost their last game to the Detroit Lions and finished the year at 0-11-1, the NFL's worst record since 1944.

Donald Perkins played running back for the Dallas Cowboys in the early 1960s.

Tackle Bob Lilly sacks Miami quarterback Bob Griese.

The next season, the Cowboys beat the Pittsburgh Steelers 27-24 on opening day before a crowd of 23,500 fans at the Cotton Bowl. Dallas scored 10 points in the game's final 56 seconds for the win. Perkins became the first Cowboy to rush for over 100 yards in a game. After the first four weeks, the Cowboys were 3-1, good for a first-place tie in the NFL's Eastern Division.

Though the Cowboys finished with a 4-9-1 record, they were getting better. Perkins was named NFL Rookie of the Year. First round draft choice Bob Lilly also emerged as a star defensive end.

In 1965, the Cowboys signed quarterback Jerry Rhome to backup Meredith. Dallas finished at 7-7 and went to the playoffs for the first time. But then they lost to the Baltimore Colts 35-3. Despite the defeat, Dallas' future seemed bright.

Roger Staubach

Over the next four years, the Cowboys racked up a combined 42-12-2 record. They made the playoffs each season and appeared in the 1966 and 1967 NFL championship games. But they would not reach the Super Bowl until Roger Staubach joined the team.

Staubach was a Cincinnati high school football star in the late 1950s. After Notre Dame failed to recruit him, he joined the Naval Academy in Annapolis, Maryland. In his sophomore year, Staubach was the number six quarterback in spring practice. In the fourth game of the season, Staubach came off the bench, passed for one touchdown, and ran for two more. The Staubach era at Navy had begun.

Head coach Tom Landry discusses game strategy with quarterback Roger Staubach.

Staubach's outstanding play his junior year earned him college football's highest honor: the Heisman Trophy. He was only the fourth junior to win the award.

When Staubach finished college, the Cowboys drafted him in the tenth round. He still had a four-year commitment with the Navy. While stationed overseas, Staubach practiced throwing passes. When he finally joined the Cowboys in 1969, Staubach was good enough to challenge Craig Morton for the starting quarterback job.

Staubach quickly helped make the Cowboys one of the best teams in the NFL. Sharing quarterback duties with Morton, Staubach and Dallas went to Super Bowl V in 1970. But Staubach stayed on the sidelines the entire game. Dallas lost 16-13 to the Baltimore Colts.

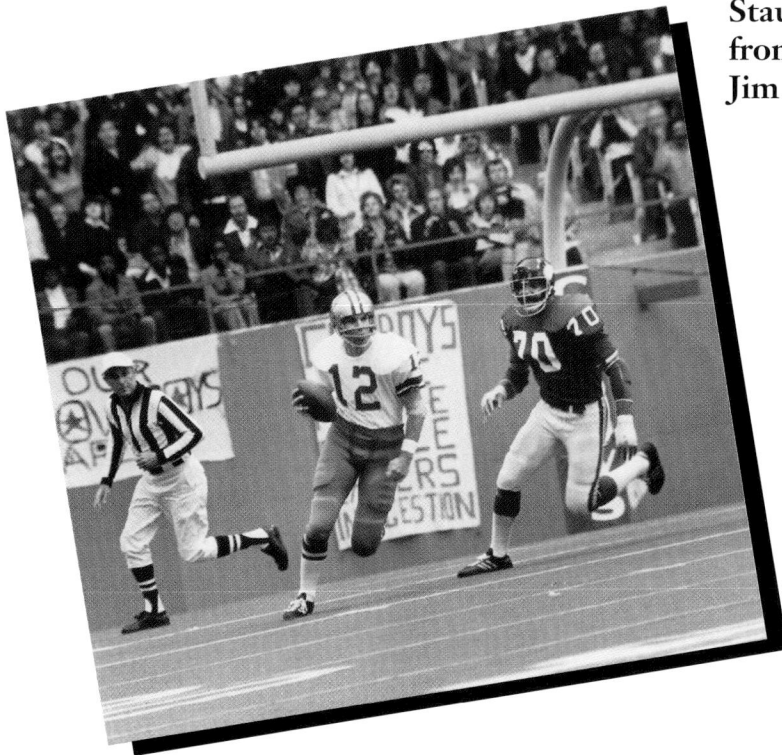

Staubach scrambles from Minnesota's Jim Marshall.

Champion Cowboys

The next year, Staubach and Morton battled for the starting quarterback job. By Week 8, Staubach had won the position. While both quarterbacks were fine passers, Staubach could also scramble for extra yardage. With the help of holdout running back Duane Thomas, who joined the team midseason, Dallas finished 7-0 to move past the Washington Redskins into first place.

Tom Landry is carried from the field after the Cowboys defeated the Miami Dolphins 24-3 in Super Bowl VI.

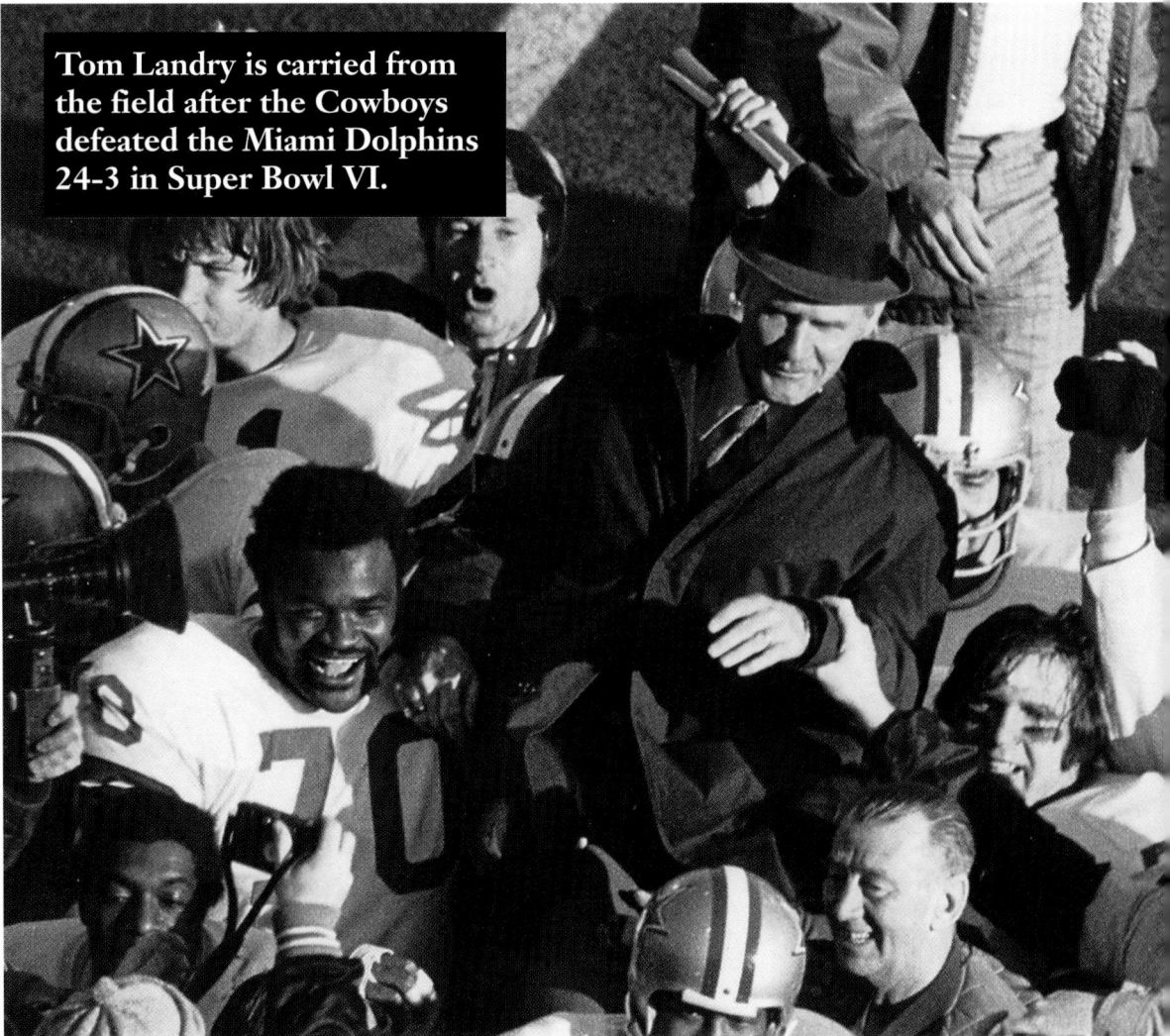

Dallas beat the San Francisco 49ers 14-3 in the NFC championship game. Then in Super Bowl VI, Dallas beat Miami 24-3 for the Cowboys' first world championship.

Staubach was named Most Valuable Player in Super Bowl VI. But the Dallas "Doomsday Defense"—Mel Renfro, Pat Toomay, George Andrie, Bob Lilly, Jethro Pugh, Dave Edwards, Lee Roy Caffey, Tom Stincic, Herb Adderley, and Larry Cole—also played well. The defense set Super Bowl records for the fewest total yards allowed (185) and the fewest touchdowns allowed (none).

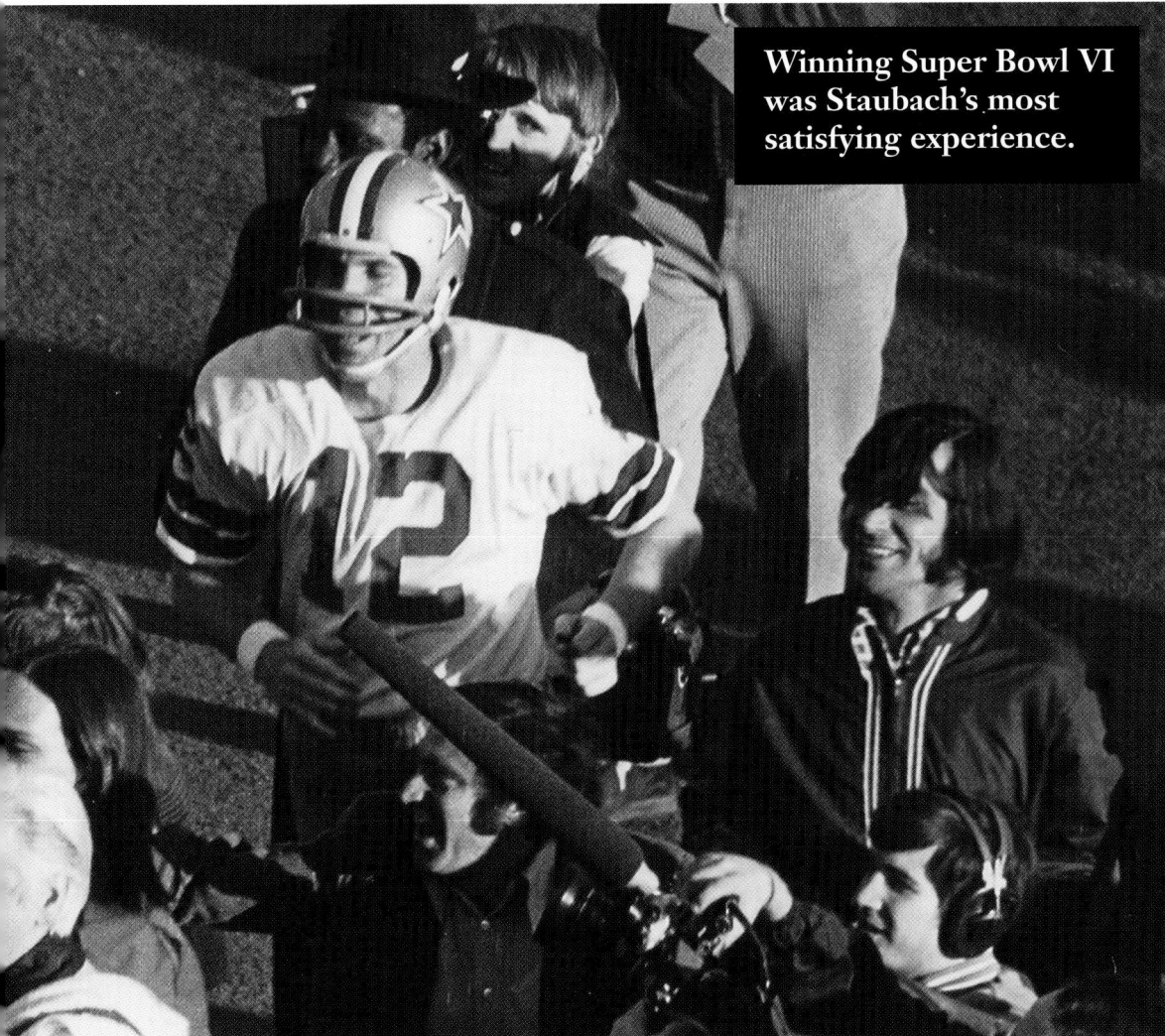

Winning Super Bowl VI was Staubach's most satisfying experience.

The First Dynasty

The Cowboys played in two more NFC championship games (1972 and 1973) and three more Super Bowls. They lost in 1975 and 1978, but won in 1977 before Staubach's retirement in 1979.

Staubach was the best quarterback the Cowboys ever had. During his career, he directed 23 comeback victories—14 of them in the last two minutes of the game or in overtime. He also led the NFL in passing in 1971, 1973, 1978, and 1979, and was named to five Pro Bowls. In 1985, he was elected to the NFL Hall of Fame.

But Dallas was not a one-man show. Running back Tony Dorsett was also responsible for much of Dallas' success during the late 1970s and early 1980s. Dorsett was a Heisman Trophy-winning running back out of the University of Pittsburgh. Dallas drafted him as the NFL's number-one pick in 1977.

Landry did not like to start rookies. But in the middle of the 1977 season, Landry realized Dorsett was the best running back he had ever coached. Dorsett started the rest of the season as the Cowboys finished 12-2 that year and won their second world championship, a 27-10 victory over the Denver Broncos.

The following season, Dorsett rushed for 1,325 yards and seven touchdowns. The Cowboys returned to the Super Bowl but lost 35-31 to the Pittsburgh Steelers.

In 1980, quarterback Danny White guided the Cowboys to a 12-4 season and two postseason victories. But Dallas lost 20-7 to the Philadelphia Eagles in the NFC championship game.

Tony Dorsett helped the Cowboys finish 12-2 in 1977 and win their second Super Bowl title.

Dallas Cowboys

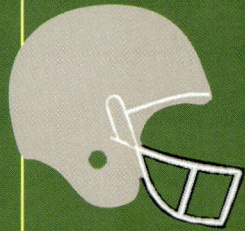

"Dandy" Don
Meredith signs with
the Cowboys in 1962.

Coach Tom Landry
leads the Cowboys
to victory in Super
Bowl VI.

Da

Cow

Don Perkins is
named NFL Rookie
of the Year in 1962.

Roger Staubach joins
the Cowboys in 1969.

40 20 10

Dallas drafts Tony Dorsett as the NFL's number-one pick in 1977.

Troy Aikman is the Cowboys' number-one draft pick in 1989.

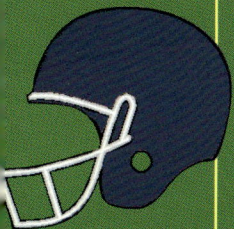

Emmitt Smith leads the NFL in rushing from 1991 to 1993.

40 30 20 10

Jimmy Johnson becomes head coach in 1989.

Dallas Cowboys

Cowboy Decline

The next season, White directed the Cowboys to the Eastern Division title and another 12-4 record. They routed the Tampa Bay Buccaneers 38-0 in the second round of the playoffs, but then lost a 28-27 heartbreaker to San Francisco in the NFC championship game.

Dallas finished second to the Redskins in the strike-shortened 1982 season. But they made the playoffs with a 6-3 record and won two playoff games to reach the NFC title game. But the Washington Redskins won 31-17.

In 1983, the Cowboys finished behind the Redskins again. In the first round of the playoffs, the Cowboys lost 24-17 to the Los Angeles Rams. Then in 1984, Drew Pearson, Harvey Martin, Pat Donovan, Billy Joe DuPree, and Robert Newhouse retired. The Cowboys dropped to 9-7 and a fourth-place finish.

The Cowboys returned to the playoffs in 1985 as the NFC East champions. But they showed signs of aging. Dorsett, Danny White, Randy White, and Ed "Too Tall" Jones were over 30 years old.

After 10 weeks, the Cowboys were 7-3. But on November 17, the Chicago Bears came to Dallas and crushed them 44-0. The loss ended the NFL's second-longest non-shutout streak at 218 games. Later in the season, the Cincinnati Bengals beat the Cowboys 50-24. In the playoffs, Dallas lost 20-0 to the L.A. Rams.

The Cowboys' decline continued for the remainder of the 1980s. Herschel Walker joined Dallas in 1986 after three years with the New Jersey Generals in the United States Football League (USFL). An outstanding player at the University of Georgia, Walker won the Heisman Trophy in his junior year. He was only the seventh junior to win the award.

When Danny White retired in 1988, he ranked second behind Roger Staubach in career passing yards.

Walker joined Dorsett in the Dallas backfield. He led the Cowboys in rushing in 1987, 1988, and 1989. But Dallas finished out of the playoff hunt each year.

By the 1988 season, Dallas traded Dorsett to the Denver Broncos. During his career with Dallas, Dorsett rushed for one thousand yards or more every year except in the 1982 strike-shortened season.

Dorsett became the Cowboy's all-time leading rusher with 12,036 yards and 72 touchdowns. He was third on the Cowboy's all-time pass receiving list with 382 passes caught for 3,432 yards. He was also second in scoring with 516 total points. Dorsett finished fourth on the NFL's all-time rushing list, behind Walter Payton, Jim Brown, and Franco Harris. He also held the NFL record for the longest run in football history, 99 yards in a Monday night game against the Minnesota Vikings in 1983.

Danny White decided to retire in 1988. He held Cowboys' records for most pass completions in a career (1,761) and most completions in a season (334). And he finished second in career passing yards behind Roger Staubach.

The Second Dynasty

Anew era in Dallas Cowboys' history began on April 18, 1989, when Jerry Jones bought the team. Jones knew that improvements had to be made. The Cowboys had been to the playoffs only once since 1984, and had had three straight losing seasons. Landry had been the only coach the Cowboys had ever had, and was very popular. But Jones wanted a fresh start. He hired his good friend, University of Miami coach Jimmy Johnson.

Johnson and Jones knew each other well. In 1964, they were co-captains of the University of Arkansas' championship team. They were also college roommates.

Johnson became head coach of the University of Miami Hurricanes in 1984. The Hurricanes finished second in the nation in 1986 and 1988. They were voted the country's top college team in 1987. Jones wanted Johnson to bring Dallas a championship. He wouldn't disappoint his old friend.

Owner Jerry Jones (right) and coach Jimmy Johnson.

Troy and Emmitt

Coach Johnson rebuilt the Cowboys in 1989. He traded Walker to Minnesota for future draft choices and a number of Vikings players. And he chose UCLA quarterback Troy Aikman as the number one college pick.

Aikman was the third-rated passer in college football history. In his first season with Dallas, he broke the league's passing record for rookies. Another Cowboys' standout that year was sixth-year linebacker Eugene Lockhart. He led the league in tackles. But these outstanding performances were not enough to lift the 1-15 Cowboys out of the NFL basement.

The following season, Dallas nearly finished with a .500 record. Their defense ranked first in the NFC in pass defense and fourth overall. Rookie running back Emmitt Smith rushed for almost 1,000 yards. And Aikman had All-Pro passing numbers. Dallas' 7-9 record helped win Johnson NFC Coach of the Year honors.

In Troy Aikman's first season with Dallas, he broke the league's passing record for rookies.

In 1991, the Cowboys made the playoffs for the first time since 1985. Emmitt Smith led the offense with an NFL-best 1,563 yards. Wide receiver Michael Irvin caught 93 passes for a league-high 1,523 yards. Aikman was the league's best quarterback until he injured his knee in Game 12. Backup Steve Beuerlein kept the team in the playoff hunt, and No. 1 draft pick Russell Maryland led the defense with his outstanding play at tackle.

The Cowboys finished second with an 11-5 record and beat the Chicago Bears 17-10 in the first playoff round. A 38-6 loss to the Detroit Lions ended their Super Bowl hopes. Though the defeat was disappointing, Dallas knew they were on the right track. The playoff experience they had gained would serve them well in the coming years. Next year, they would not accept defeat.

In 1991, Emmitt Smith won his first rushing title.

A Remarkable Comeback

In 1992, the Cowboys accomplished one of the most remarkable comebacks in NFL history. They went from 1-15 in 1989 to 13-3 in 1992—ending the season with a Super Bowl championship. Aikman passed for 23 touchdowns and was the Super Bowl MVP. Smith led the NFL in rushing with 1,713 yards and 19 touchdowns. Irvin caught 78 passes for 1,396 yards and seven scores. And Jay Novacek led the NFL's tight ends with 68 catches. Even more, the Cowboys had the league's best defense—even though none of the defensive players made the Pro Bowl. Defensive end Charles Haley and defensive back Thomas Everett were among the defensive stars.

In the playoffs, Dallas routed the Philadelphia Eagles 34-10 in the second round. Then in the NFC championship game, the Cowboys earned their first Super Bowl appearance in 14 years with a 30-20 victory over the 49ers in San Francisco.

Alvin Harper (left) and Michael Irvin raise their arms in victory after the Cowboys beat the Buffalo Bills in Super Bowl XXVII.

Jerry Jones and Jimmy Johnson hold up the Vince Lombardi Trophy as they celebrate their first Super Bowl win.

The Cowboys' 52-17 win over the Buffalo Bills in Super Bowl XXVII marked the beginning of another Dallas dynasty. The game was close until just before halftime. Then Dallas turned an uneasy 14-10 lead into a 28-10 rout that continued throughout the second half. Aikman threw for touchdown passes on 22-of-30 passing for 273 yards and no interceptions. He threw touchdown passes of 18 and 19 yards to Irvin, 23 yards to Novacek, and 45 yards to Alvin Harper. Smith rushed for 108 yards on 22 carries and scored on a 10-yard run.

But the Dallas defense was the real star. Defensive end Jimmie Jones scored on a two-yard fumble return, and linebacker Ken Norton ended the scoring on a nine-yard fumble return. Dallas' margin of victory was the third-largest in Super Bowl history.

In 1993, the Cowboys became the fifth team to win back-to-back Super Bowls. This time it was Emmitt Smith's turn to shine. He was named the NFL's Most Valuable Player and the Super Bowl MVP. Smith rushed for 1,486 yards to lead the NFL for the third straight year.

The Cowboys won the Eastern Division with a 12-4 record. They rolled over the Green Bay Packers (27-17) and the 49ers (38-21) in the playoffs before facing the Bills again in the Super Bowl. This time they won 30-13. But it wasn't that easy.

Buffalo led 13-6 at halftime. In the third quarter, they were driving for another score. That's when backup safety James Washington made the play of the game. Dallas defensive end Leon Lett stripped the ball from Buffalo running back Thurman Thomas. Washington scooped it up and ran 46 yards for the tying score.

Following Washington's touchdown, Smith took over. He carried the ball seven out of eight plays and scored on a 15-yard run. In the fourth quarter, Smith scored from one yard out.

For the game, Smith rushed for 132 yards on 30 carries and scored two touchdowns—while playing with a separated shoulder. The Cowboys' fourth Super Bowl victory tied a record held by Pittsburgh and San Francisco. Their seventh overall appearance set another record.

Trouble in Dallas

All seemed well in Dallas after the second-consecutive Super Bowl win. But trouble was brewing. Jimmy Johnson and Jerry Jones were fighting for control of the team. Being the owner, Jones won the battle, and Johnson resigned.

Jones hired former University of Oklahoma football coach Barry Switzer. Dallas didn't seem to skip a beat as they won their first two games of the 1994 season. By Week 10, Dallas was 8-1 and in first place in the NFC East. After a 21-14 loss to San Francisco in Week 11, Dallas won another three in a row before losing 19-14 to Cleveland in Week 15. Dallas finished the season with a 12-4 record and a first-place finish in the NFC East.

In the playoffs, Dallas rode Troy Aikman's arm to a 35-9 victory over Green Bay. Smith left the game late in the first quarter with a hamstring injury. But Aikman passed for two touchdowns and a club playoff record 337 yards, including a 94-yard touchdown strike to Harper—the longest offensive touchdown in NFL playoff history.

Harper (108 yards) was one of three Dallas receivers with more than 100 yards. Irvin had 111 and Novacek had 104. Novacek's 11 catches set a Dallas playoff record. Blair Thomas replaced Emmitt Smith and rushed for 70 yards and two touchdowns.

But the Dallas dynasty was derailed in the NFC championship game against the 49ers. San Francisco, which lost to Dallas in the championship game the past two seasons, streaked to a 21-0 lead halfway through the first quarter. The 49ers then hung on to defeat the two-time Super Bowl champions 38-28.

Dallas receiver Michael Irvin takes off from the line during the 1994 NFC championship game against the 49ers.

Dallas was trying to become the first team to win three consecutive Super Bowls. But five turnovers ruined their chances. The first three set up the 49ers first 21 points in the game's first 7 minutes 27 seconds. Dallas never got closer than 10 points, despite a 380-yard passing day by Aikman, and a club playoff-record 12 catches for 192 yards, plus 2 touchdowns by Michael Irvin. Smith rushed for 74 yards and 2 scores before he pulled his right hamstring early in the fourth quarter.

Back On Track

Though Dallas did not win the championship, it was only a minor setback. During the offseason, Smith healed his injuries while Jones signed superstar defensive back Deion Sanders to a huge contract. With most of their weaknesses cured, Dallas took aim at another championship. They still have the youth, talent, and experience to return to the Super Bowl and win it all—for many years to come.

Deion Sanders joined the Cowboys in 1995.

GLOSSARY

ALL-PRO—A player who is voted to the Pro Bowl.

BACKFIELD—Players whose position is behind the line of scrimmage.

CORNERBACK—Either of two defensive halfbacks stationed a short distance behind the linebackers and relatively near the sidelines.

DEFENSIVE END—A defensive player who plays on the end of the line and often next to the defensive tackle.

DEFENSIVE TACKLE—A defensive player who plays on the line and between the guard and end.

ELIGIBLE—A player who is qualified to be voted into the Hall of Fame.

END ZONE—The area on either end of a football field where players score touchdowns.

EXTRA POINT—The additional one-point score added after a player makes a touchdown. Teams earn an extra point if the placekicker kicks the ball through the uprights of the goalpost.

FIELD GOAL—A three-point score awarded when a placekicker kicks the ball through the uprights of the goalpost.

FULLBACK—An offensive player who often lines up farthest behind the front line.

FUMBLE—When a player loses control of the football.

GUARD—An offensive lineman who plays between the tackles and center.

GROUND GAME—The running game.

HALFBACK—An offensive player whose position is behind the line of scrimmage.

HALFTIME—The time period between the second and third quarters of a football game.

INTERCEPTION—When a defensive player catches a pass from an offensive player.

KICK RETURNER—An offensive player who returns kickoffs.

LINEBACKER—A defensive player whose position is behind the line of scrimmage.

LINEMAN—An offensive or defensive player who plays on the line of scrimmage.

PASS—To throw the ball.

PASS RECEIVER—An offensive player who runs pass routes and catches passes.

PLACEKICKER—An offensive player who kicks extra points and field goals. The placekicker also kicks the ball from a tee to the opponent after his team has scored.

PLAYOFFS—The postseason games played amongst the division winners and wild card teams which determines the Super Bowl champion.

PRO BOWL—The postseason All-Star game which showcases the NFL's best players.

PUNT—To kick the ball to the opponent.

QUARTER—One of four 15-minute time periods that makes up a football game.

QUARTERBACK—The backfield player who usually calls the signals for the plays.

REGULAR SEASON—The games played after the preseason and before the playoffs.

ROOKIE—A first-year player.

RUNNING BACK—A backfield player who usually runs with the ball.

RUSH—To run with the football.

SACK—To tackle the quarterback behind the line of scrimmage.

SAFETY—A defensive back who plays behind the linemen and linebackers. Also, two points awarded for tackling an offensive player in his own end zone when he's carrying the ball.

SPECIAL TEAMS—Squads of football players that perform special tasks (for example, kickoff team and punt-return team).

SPONSOR—A person or company that finances a football team.

SUPER BOWL—The NFL championship game played between the AFC champion and the NFC champion.

T FORMATION—An offensive formation in which the fullback lines up behind the center and quarterback with one halfback stationed on each side of the fullback.

TACKLE—An offensive or defensive lineman who plays between the ends and the guards.

TAILBACK—The offensive back farthest from the line of scrimmage.

TIGHT END—An offensive lineman who is stationed next to the tackles, and who usually blocks or catches passes.

TOUCHDOWN—When one team crosses the goal line of the other team's end zone. A touchdown is worth six points.

TURNOVER—To turn the ball over to an opponent either by a fumble, an interception, or on downs.

TWO-POINT CONVERSION—The additional two points scored after a player makes a touchdown. Teams earn the extra two points if an offensive player crosses the goal line with the football before being tackled.

UNDERDOG—The team that is picked to lose the game.

WIDE RECEIVER—An offensive player who is stationed relatively close to the sidelines and who usually catches passes.

WILD CARD—A team that makes the playoffs without winning its division.

ZONE PASS DEFENSE—A pass defense method where defensive backs defend a certain area of the playing field rather than individual pass receivers.

INDEX